Heard

Reflections on the story of Hannah

by

F.T. Briones

Foreword by
Pastor Bryan Jacobs

To Hannah

Table of Contents

Foreword

by Pastor Bryan Jacobs

When people pray, they may wonder if there's anyone really listening. Have their requests and worries been heard, or are they simply echoes in a lonely bedroom? The Bible assures believers that God does in fact hear their prayers. Scripture says, "*the eyes of the Lord are on the righteous, and his ears are open to their prayer*" (1 Peter 3:12, ESV). In another place, the Bible says, "*When the righteous cry for help, the Lord hears*" (Psalm 34:17, ESV). If you are a believer, Scripture promises that you are heard. This blessing is for all those who have put their trust in Jesus Christ alone to save them from their sins.

By reading *Heard: Reflections on the Story of Hannah*, I believe you will gain a greater assurance that God loves you and hears you. In Farah's book, she skillfully examines the biblical story of Hannah to find modern life applications for you and me. As you'll see, Hannah's life teaches us the value of faith in God's sovereign care. Farah will help you to understand your relationship with God more deeply through her faithfulness to Scripture and her personal reflections on this lesson.

Having known Farah and her family for years as members of our church, I have seen firsthand their humble trust in God's care. Their confidence in God's love has brought them peace even in the most challenging times. I pray that you too will gain a confidence in God's loving concern for you through Farah's words in this book.

Introduction

I started writing this book around the time that my daughter, Hannah, started to take on the great challenge of college applications. She was learning first-hand about the importance of crafting a good introduction. We attended many information sessions hosted by different colleges. In each of them the admissions counselor often points out that what they want is to be able to get to know the prospective student in their application and essay to see if they will be a "good fit." Hearing this statement repeated several times as we went through this process with our Hannah, I was reminded of just how often people who don't know us try to size us up according to a very limited amount of information.

As it was true for Hannah in the Old Testament, so it is true for our Hannah, and true for all of us today. We are all too often judged using only observable information. Sometimes, digging a little deeper allows people to know us better, but it never assures us of acceptance or even understanding. What a comfort it is then to know that *"…the Lord sees not as man sees: man looks on the outward appearance, but the Lord looks on the heart."*[1]

Asking for God's guidance, I wrote this book in hopes that I can share this all-important and overarching theme from the story of Hannah in the book of Samuel. Our heart is where God communes with us. He sees our hearts. He hears our hearts. There is nothing in our hearts that is hidden from Him.

Yet, even as I write this, I quickly realize that the idea of God knowing our hearts so intimately may be a comfort to some but not others. Hard as it may be to admit, we often are actually more pre-occupied with having our outer appearance look better than our hearts. Such is the foolishness that many of us embark on at some or several points in our lives. We try to look attractive to others and even to ourselves on the outside. We forget that God's are the one set of eyes that matter most when it comes to evaluating our real worth, and His eyes look straight into our hearts.

---

[1] 1 Samuel 16:7 (ESV)

God knows us – our history, our family, our current situation. Hannah in the book of 1 Samuel may have been embarrassed to introduce herself to others because of her perceived inadequacies, but she could've found her value in what God had done for her instead of how people evaluated her. God knows us even better than we know ourselves and still loves us. He sees us and welcomes us. He hears our hearts, even before we may have even uttered a single word.

So, with this book I pray that you will walk with me slowly, thoughtfully, and with a constant eye toward God's personal messages to you through the story of Hannah. This woman whose character lives up to her name has been given a story to help the rest of us understand God's unrelenting love and attention to our hearts.

Hannah's story echoes a recurring theme in scripture that God's love endures forever. The Message translation of Psalm 136 I believe renders this point so clearly –
"God remembered us when we were down,
   His love never quits.
Rescued us from the trampling boot,
   His love never quits.

Takes care of everyone in time of need.
   His love never quits.
Thank God, who did it all!
   His love never quits!"[2]

God's loving guidance and perfect timing of deliverance, sustenance and grace has always been something I have marveled at. Even in the writing of this book, I saw how God's timing is always correct. As I was approaching the homestretch in the completion of this project, the world was thrown into lockdown due to the threat of the COVID-19 pandemic. While I continue to pray for God's healing for those who became ill, comfort for the families who may have lost loved ones, and deliverance of the countries that were most affected by this virus, I rejoice in the assurance that God has not and will never stop loving us. I am thankful that even in these current times of darkness and seeming hopelessness, He speaks to us through His word and through the stories of great men and women of faith, like Hannah.

---

[2] Psalm 136:23-26 The Message

I pray that in going through this book, God will be as real in your life as He was in Hannah's life. No matter what darkness, loneliness or seeming despair may surround you, you can be sure your heart is never beyond God's sight and hearing. His love for you never quits.

Real roots

¹ There was a certain man of Ramathaim-zophim of the hill country of Ephraim whose name was Elkanah the son of Jeroham, son of Elihu, son of Tohu, son of Zuph, an Ephrathite. ² He had two wives. The name of the one was Hannah, and the name of the other, Peninnah. And Peninnah had children, but Hannah had no children.
1 Samuel 1:1-2 ESV

Have you ever struggled with introducing yourself? Especially in those times when you feel it may matter more than at any other time-- in job interviews, a first date, or in a college essay for example-- having a good grasp of who you are in terms of where you came from and how you are currently doing in life is immensely important. Sometimes, even more important than having a good handle on who we are is being able to present ourselves in such a way as to make the best first impression. But what if you think there is nothing very impressive about you at the moment? Maybe you had dropped out of school for reasons beyond your control. Maybe you've been trying so hard to get your business off the ground, but nothing seems to work, and you ultimately had to close up shop. Maybe you've been trying your best to save your marriage or set your child on the right course, but the harder you try to pull everyone together, the stronger they seem to pull the other way. You know you were called to do great things, but now it seems even the little things are beyond your reach.

Hannah, one of the main characters at the beginning of the book of 1 Samuel, is given an introduction that speaks of who she is and how she has fared in life so far. We may assume from these opening verses that Hannah would have received her calling early in life. She was to be the wife of a man devoted to God, from a family that is historically significant to her nation, Israel. Her husband, Elkanah, is descended from the sons of Korah, from the tribe of Levi who have been especially appointed by God to serve as priests and lead His people in worship. She was part of a very important family, holding a God-appointed position in the nation. However, not everything about this family line may be considered *distinguished*. There is a time in their history when divine punishment fell upon the tribe. Korah, forefather of Hannah's husband, Elkanah, was one of 249 Israelites who rebelled against Moses and Aaron. We read in the Book of Numbers that their rebellion displeased God and these 249 men were swallowed up by the earth as punishment[3]. It is this same history that we can assume Elkanah's family looks back to as they worship the God who has time and again shown himself as Almighty and worthy of worship. In that part of Elkanah's history, not only does his family

---

[3] Numbers 16:1-40

(which here includes his wife, Hannah) have a specific event to which they can look back and see more than enough reason to worship and fear God, but also the reason to believe in His mercy and rejoice in it. As history records and their own existence proves, it was only by God's grace and mercy that the sons of Korah did not die[4], and so the family line was able to continue.

To be part of a family with such roots is truly a God-given calling. This was Hannah's calling—to be the wife of a man set apart for priestly work, and to continue this family line by bearing and raising his children. Sadly, Hannah was unable to fulfill the second part of her calling—or at least not right away. Hannah did not have any children, and so she had to deal with the presence of another wife who could bear children for her husband. This sets the stage for us as we begin to get to know Hannah—a woman whose performance so far, based on the culture at the time, is not very impressive. Nevertheless, God chose Hannah to occupy this particular place in history and gave her real roots with her husband Elkanah. Strong roots.

---

[4] Numbers 26:11

9

These roots can be traced back all the way to Levi, one of the patriarchs of the 12 tribes of Israel, whose calling came from no other than the Almighty, merciful, gracious God-of-the-angel-armies.

In this short introduction of Hannah, an unpopular and counter-cultural lesson emerges for us. The lesson is this: The source of our worth is God. Our worth does not come from what we can accomplish on our own, which can be unreliable and unpredictable. My worth does not depend on how much money I make, how my children behave, how many wedding anniversaries my husband and I can celebrate together, or whatever other metric the world may want to use. It would certainly be good to make enough money to live in big house, to have children that other parents wished they had, to have the ideal spouse and an unbreakable marriage. But it is also good to know that we are imperfect people, just like every other person in our lives. Because of this imperfection in all of us, we can only expect that life will surely hold a certain level of brokenness, a certain degree of imperfection, which will require a great dependence on God who alone can perfectly love and care for us.

Hannah was barren, but God made her part of a family tree which contained a wonderful testimony to God's grace. Therefore, even when we may feel inadequate by cultural standards, we can find our worth in God.[5] No matter the historical context, the societal norms, or even our own view of ourselves, God gives us our worth. In this alone, we have reason to keep our head held high with joy, yet also bowed low with humility and gratitude to our God without whom we are nothing.

---

[5] Pastor Bryan Jacobs, July 19, 2019

Think: Have you ever felt misjudged by others? How can a deeper understanding of God's presence in your life, and the worth that you have in Him, affect your response in such situations?

Pray: Lord, thank you for giving me worth that is rooted in your love and grace, and not in what I or others may think about me.

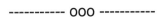

----------- OOO -----------

Heard
Reflections on the story of Hannah

Vertical view

³ Now this man used to go up year by year from his city to worship and to sacrifice to the Lord of hosts at Shiloh, where the two sons of Eli, Hophni and Phinehas, were priests of the Lord. ⁴ On the day when Elkanah sacrificed, he would give portions to Peninnah his wife and to all her sons and daughters. ⁵ But to Hannah he gave a double portion, because he loved her, though the Lord had closed her womb.
1 Samuel 1:3-5 ESV

I feel for Hannah. Year after year, her husband and his whole family took this special trip. It was a sacred yet very public tradition. One that must have made her even more aware of her inadequacies as she would openly have to stand beside her husband and his children (none of whom belonged to her), together with their mother (the other wife). We can only assume and imagine that there are great feelings of pain within Hannah, feelings of hurt against her husband for having put her in the middle of a polygamous marriage. She may even be blaming herself for her inability to bear children for him.

As Hannah found only disappointment when she looked at herself and at her husband, she may have sought hope and solace at the temple. Yet even there, people let her down. The two priests, Hophni and Phinehas, did not live up to their calling as priests. These "*sons of Eli were worthless men. They did not know the Lord.*"[6] Furthermore, the historical setting for the books of Samuel is during that time when the whole nation was living in sin and rebellion against God. The story of Hannah

---

[6] 1 Samuel 2:12

happened at the tail-end of the time when priests served as Judges over Israel, but none of them were doing a good job. "*In those days there was no king in Israel; everyone did what was right in his own eyes.*"[7]

These were dark times for Hannah. She was frustrated with her circumstances in life. She may be disappointed in herself and in the person closest to her, her husband, Elkanah. She was let down by people who were supposed to be leaders in her community-- the priests Hophni and Phinehas-- those whom she ought to have been able to look up to but could not.

I can only suppose that what enabled Hannah to go to this family event year after year was a silent determination in her heart to focus on God and not on those around her. They were, after all, going to the temple to worship the Lord of hosts, God-of-the-angel-armies. He is Almighty God who is worthy of her sacrifice, and of her worship. Truly she could only look up to God, and in doing so, God sustained her. The vertical view was the only one that could show her hope in the dark times in her life.

---

[7] Judges 21:25

In the middle of all this, we know that God sees and hears Hannah's heart. It is worth noting here that while Elkanah, her husband had his shortcomings, God still used him to be a channel of love and comfort to Hannah. As he worshiped God and performed his duties with everyone in the family, Elkanah's heart was moved to show an extra ounce of love to Hannah.[8] Even in this simple gesture through Elkanah, God assures Hannah that He cares for her. How wonderful it is when we see reflections of God, and feel His arms embrace us through the expressions of love that we receive from those that He placed in our lives!

Like Hannah, I am also a full-time wife and mother. Like her, I too have inadequacies that I struggle with. I am aware of how people size up one another, and I feel there are areas where I am certainly found lacking. Yet, like Hannah, I also go to worship the Lord with my family regularly. As part of the team that leads the church in worship, I am onstage with my family on a pretty regular basis, and this often makes me feel like my inadequacies are in the spotlight. There is nowhere to hide

---

[8] 1 Samuel 1:4-5

whether I am up onstage or not. Nonetheless, I keep going week after week having decided in my heart that I will focus on God and depend only on His strength and grace. We do, after all, go to church to worship the Lord of hosts, God-of-the-angel-armies. Strangely enough, the spotlight on my inadequacies grows dim and the light on the Lord gets brighter when I choose to focus on Him.

Also, like Hannah, I know that the Lord hears my heart. He sees and hears me struggle with the insecurities built over years of struggling to overcome physical limitations, of trying harder than most even to just appear "normal." God, in His infinite wisdom surrounded me with just the right people to be His arms to hold me up and embrace me especially at the times when He knows I need it most.

All of us are blessed by God with imperfection. Imperfect selves, imperfect families, imperfect leaders – all of us living in an imperfect world. Yes, these are all blessings. In much the same way as those who mourn are blessed because they will be comforted[9], we are blessed with the imperfections

---

[9] Matthew 5:4

of life because it gives us cause to look up to the only One who is perfect and in whom we find true hope and joy. As sunshine looks even brighter when we come out to it from a dark place, so much greater is the joy we feel when we look up to God after having spent so much time seeing only the sad state of our lives.

Think: How do your current circumstances, and the people who surround you, affect the way you see your life and future?

Pray: Lord, teach the eyes of my heart not to dwell on the imperfect within and around me, but to choose to focus on you, and find joy and peace in your perfect love and care for me.

----------- ooo -----------

Heard
Reflections on the story of Hannah

Persistent pain

6 And her rival used to provoke her grievously to irritate her, because the Lord had closed her womb.
7 So it went on year by year. As often as she went up to the house of the Lord, she used to provoke her. Therefore Hannah wept and would not eat. 8 And Elkanah, her husband, said to her, "Hannah, why do you weep? And why do you not eat? And why is your heart sad? Am I not more to you than ten sons?"
1 Samuel 1:6-8 ESV

Bullies. We all have them in our lives. Those that make it their mission to show us how miserably we've failed, how small we are, or how our life can never be better than how it currently is. Sometimes these bullies are what we may call, as the Apostle Paul called it, a *thorn in the flesh*[10].

Sometimes these thorns in the flesh are not people but inabilities, insecurities, or past mistakes that we just can't seem to get over or rectify no matter how hard we try. They come back to haunt us and cause us persistent pain.

Hannah's rival, Penninah, is her bully; her thorn in the flesh who provoked her to *grievously irritate her*. This went on year by year, as often as they did their yearly visit to the house of the Lord. She made it her mission to remind Hannah of her inability to have children, and of how this makes Hannah a failure as a wife and mother.

The pain that Penninah caused Hannah was not only persistent but, more so, intense. The bullying beat on Hannah's heart and mind so much that it

---

[10] 2 Corinthians 12:7

caused Hannah to cry and not want to eat. Is there anyone or anything in your life that has ever made you feel this way? Like Hannah, you may feel like the bullying you feel in your heart is never going to end. The bully in your life may make you feel like accepting defeat and just trying to get on from one day to the next, carrying the burden of your being not enough of one thing or too much of another. You may be at the brink of agreeing with and believing your bully's lies-- *Maybe you're too nice, or you're not nice enough. You're too fat, or you're too thin. You're not smart enough, or you're too smart.* The taunting and jeering can sometimes seem too much to bear.

Interestingly, these "thorns" in our life, are like thorns on the stem of a rose. While painfully sharp, they are quite small. But the more we focus on them, the more they occupy our field of vision and the more gigantic they seem to be than they actually are. They become disproportionately larger than everything else in our life, until someone comes along to jolt us back to our senses. Just as in this part of Hannah's story, Elkanah breaks through Hannah's momentary myopia and asks, *"And why is your heart sad? Am I not more to you than ten sons?"* In today's language he might have said, *"Hey, Hannah! I'm still here. Don't I matter?"* How often have we allowed ourselves to wallow in our own concerns that we forget the people that God surrounds us with? Have you ever allowed your concerns to take over so much of your life and attention that it makes you forget that you are truly *not* alone? Have you focused so long and so closely at your imperfections that it has made you unable to see everything else around you?

The bullies in our lives are like the proverbial ink blot on a blank sheet of paper. Picture it – one dot in the middle of a clean page. It's always easier to focus on the ink blot rather than the immense, clean, promising space that still exists. Human nature makes it difficult to shift our focus. Thankfully, God comes to our rescue and enables us to see what we could so easily miss when we rely only on our strength and vision. He surrounds us with people to remind us how small the ink blot is, and how much more there is to life than our own inabilities and momentary suffering.

Life's pains and sorrows sometimes seem like they will never end. There can be challenges, annoyances, and hurdles that persist in our lives, but there is One who is more constant than any of these. Our God who hears the cries of our heart is faithful, and He asks us to trust and love Him even through all of life's pains. In loving Him and communing with Him, we find the unexplainable joy and peace that surpasses all human understanding.[11]

---

[11] Philippians 4:6-7

Think: The best cure for persistent pain is constant closeness with God.

Pray: Lord, please grow in me the desire to stay close to you. Please grow my strength and wisdom to recognize persistent lies that try to bully me and rob me of the joy and fullness of life that you promised, and indeed, have already so generously given me.

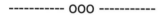

----------- ooo -----------

Rest and rise

⁹ After they had eaten and drunk in Shiloh, Hannah rose. Now Eli the priest was sitting on the seat beside the doorpost of the temple of the Lord. ¹⁰ She was deeply distressed and prayed to the Lord and wept bitterly.
1 Samuel 1:9-10 ESV

Have you ever wished there was a *pause* button for life? Maybe we could call it the *Life-pause App*. We can download it onto our phones and we can pause everything around us for a little while whenever we wanted. For those times when I look at my children and think to myself, "I wish they would stay this young and close to me just a little longer," I would pull up the *Life-pause* app, and I would press the pause button right then so I can savor the moment a few more minutes. The same goes for those times when life is especially challenging. When I'm supposed to get something done and there's just not enough time to do it, that *Life-pause* app would surely come in handy.

That *Life-pause* app or *Life-pause* button does not exist, but something real and more dependable does. God, our Heavenly Father, gives us peace and rest no matter where we are or what our circumstances might be. We need only to *choose* to pause and wait on Him. As King David said in the Psalms, we can also say as a child of God, "*For*

God alone, O my soul, wait in silence, for my hope is from him."[12]

In Hannah's story, we saw the nature of her pain in the beginning verses of the book of Samuel. She hurts deeply, yet life around her isn't slowing down. She continues to struggle with meeting social obligations even when she knows that those are occasions which make her especially vulnerable to ridicule and criticism. Hannah knows in her heart that she is called to be a mother, but she is in anguish because she is yet unable to become one. She is ridiculed as an "unaccomplished mother," and is most likely made fun of because of her faith. She is in dire need of a respite. She needs to pause, and she chooses to do so in exactly the right place – in the presence of her Lord.

She continues to believe that God hears her prayer asking for the privilege of motherhood, despite the lack of any indication that she can bear a child in the future. All Hannah had were the sure words of God, and all the times in the past when she had seen how God listened to the prayers of His

---

[12] Psalm 62:5

children and answered them. Hannah held on to these with all the faith she could muster. How much faith do you think it took for Hannah to believe that God will hear, and act, and do mighty things?

In the New Testament book of Matthew, [13] Jesus reminded His followers that all that's really needed for mighty things to happen in our lives is a little faith, even if it's just the size of a mustard seed.[14] Only God knows how much faith was in Hannah's heart, just as only He knows how much faith is in our hearts when we pray. Yet like Hannah, not only can we be assured that He hears our request, we can also be sure that He will provide the pause that we need to have peace and rest as we wait for Him to move the mountains in our lives.

In verses 9 and 10 we see that Hannah has just come from a social gathering where she has had to put on a brave face despite what was going on insider her. Hannah's heart was tired, but she has decided to believe in God with whom all things are possible. She also believed in God's comfort; and

---

[13] Matthew 17:20
[14] Mustard seeds are usually 0.039 to 0.079 inches in diameter

so, she came to Him, as a child to her Father, and wept as she continued to pray and believe God would hear and answer. Hannah chose to bring her tired self to God's house, knowing that only He can truly renew her strength and cause her to rise and keep on going.

Hannah, even though she lived so long ago in history, was like us. She had to deal with public life while battling private pain. Today, you might see people like Hannah at a friend's wedding reception, trying their best to not get everyone else's spirits down; or sitting at the table during Thanksgiving dinner, wearing a big smile while dreading the pain that they'll have to keep facing after all the festivities are over. Maybe that person is you. If you're that person, choose to pause *now*. Go to God knowing that you are heard by Him. Like Hannah, He hears you, He loves you, and He welcomes you to rest in His sanctuary. As His child, if you have asked Jesus to be your Lord and savior, God's sanctuary is as close as your heart. You may not have a *Life-pause app*, but you have a Heavenly Father in whom you can rest.

God knows when we are hurting and He gives us opportunities to rest and recover. While our troubles may not all at once be taken away, He welcomes us into His presence where tears can flow, and our hearts can commune intimately with Him and be strengthened to rise and face all that may lie ahead.

Think: All we need is a fraction of an inch of faith to see mighty things happen in our lives.

Pray: Lord, help me to choose to pause and rest in the promise that You are listening and doing mighty things in my life.

----------- OOO -----------

Heard
Reflections on the story of Hannah

Ours to give

> [11] *And she vowed a vow and said, "O Lord of hosts, if you will indeed look on the affliction of your servant and remember me and not forget your servant, but will give to your servant a son, then I will give him to the Lord all the days of his life, and no razor shall touch his head."*
> *1 Samuel 1:11 ESV*

In the first 10 verses of the story of Hannah, we are allowed glimpses into her sorrow and pain. We know that there must be prayers in her heart that only God can hear. We heard the voice of her husband Elkanah, trying to refocus her attention away from her sadness in verse 8. Yet, we do not read any of Hannah's own spoken words until this point. For the first time, we hear Hannah's prayer to God and we see her utter humility.

Nothing speaks of humility more than nothingness. Hannah in this one verse alone refers to herself three times as a *servant*. A servant is someone who owns little or nothing, is a master of no one, and is one whose only purpose is to obey the biddings of the master. She made a point of stating three times that she was God's *servant*. This implies not just her having nothing, but also that she was nothing apart from God, her Master.

Curiously, Hannah in humility also confidently vows to offer something to God. How can a servant who has nothing have the boldness to promise to offer anything? The answer to this question takes me back to the story of Abraham and Isaac in Genesis, when God asked Abraham to offer Isaac as a sacrifice to Him. Abraham acted in faith and obedience even though God had just given Isaac to Abraham and his wife Sarah in their old age,[15] and it seemed to contradict God's promise to make Abraham the father of a multitude of nations.[16] Abraham believed that all he had came from God, and that God provides for everything – including even the sacrifice that He requires.[17]

In faith and humility, Hannah, like Abraham, believed that God will hear and answer her, and that God will provide something that she could offer back to God. In essence she cries for help, asks in humility, and responds in faith and with thankfulness that the Almighty God will provide according to His will. This picture of faith and humility stands in stark contrast to how people sometimes think that they can coax God into a favorable response by giving Him something in exchange.

---

[15] Genesis 21:1-3
[16] Genesis 17:1-8
[17] Genesis 22:8

At different points in my life, I have met people who at one point or another, have so desperately needed answers to their prayer requests. The level of desperation varies from one individual to the next, but those most desperate sometimes end up making a promise to give up something precious to them believing that God would somehow take notice and give in to their request. One example that comes to mind is of a beautiful young girl I knew many years ago. Her grandmother had become gravely ill and everyone in their large family committed to prayer vigils or novenas to ask God to extend her grandmother's life. One morning at school, her whole class was shocked to see that her long, beautiful, black hair had been cut to a very short bob. When asked about the sudden change in her hairstyle (since everyone knew how she loved and took care of her long hair), she said that she and her cousins offered their hair as their personal sacrifice so that God would heal their grandmother.

Something in me, even as a young girl, knew that God couldn't be manipulated in that way. I was sad for my friend and for the loss and grief that her family went through. Yet even sadder is the way that people sometimes fail to realize that trying to "bribe" God with a "sacrifice" so that He would grant their requests ultimately demonstrates a lack of faith in God's love and sovereignty. Such actions, even when done with sincerity and good intentions, actually reveal pride. When we think that we have something we can give to God that will make Him want to move in our favor, we are effectively saying, *"God, here's something that is mine. I'm sacrificing it to you as payment for this favor that I need."* How displeasing it must be to God when we do such things to try and earn His favor, when He in fact is the source of all that we may think we own.

In contrast, Hannah's vow to God in this verse recognizes both God's provision and His sovereignty. She didn't even attempt to promise to give God anything she may have currently had in her possession. Hannah knew that God is God, and He shows mercy and grace because of who He is, not because of anything we've done. It is this same principle that we see God demonstrate in sending Jesus to die for our sins in order to bring us back to Him, even though we don't deserve His forgiveness. *"...He saved us, not because of works done by us in righteousness, but according to his own mercy...*"[18]

Hannah acknowledged God's power to save her from her desperate state, and she promised God that the son He would give her would be given back to Him-- set apart and dedicated to His service.[19] Surely, what God gives would be good and pleasing to Him, and so this son from God would be the best way she could thank God for hearing and answering her prayer.

Hannah, in this short prayer, acknowledged the great power of the Lord of Hosts-- the God of the Angel Armies, and clearly conveyed a deep personal relationship with Him. Hannah knew God to be almighty and able to do anything that people may think to be impossible. Yet she also knew God as her heavenly Father -- compassionate, loving, and personally interested in each of the lives of His children.

---

[18] Titus 3:5

[19] The Nazirite's uncut hair would be a sign to all that he was consecrated, set apart, to the Lord (Baldwin, *1 and 2 Samuel,* 52). The Moody Bible Commentary © 2014, p. 405.

Knowing that God will answer her prayer, she was prepared to make an offering. Hannah's future promise reflected her present faith, and her humble vow showed not an ounce of pride or self-reliance, but her full dependence on God and faith in Him. Like Hannah, we can trust God to hear us, answer us, provide all that we need, and enable us to give back to Him.

Think: There is nothing we can give God that He hasn't first given to us.

Pray: Lord, from what you have given to me so generously, help me to offer back to you in humility.

----------- ooo -----------

Prayer perceptions

¹² As she continued praying before the Lord, Eli observed her mouth. ¹³ Hannah was speaking in her heart; only her lips moved, and her voice was not heard. Therefore Eli took her to be a drunken woman. ¹⁴ And Eli said to her, "How long will you go on being drunk? Put your wine away from you." ¹⁵ But Hannah answered, "No, my lord, I am a woman troubled in spirit. I have drunk neither wine nor strong drink, but I have been pouring out my soul before the Lord. ¹⁶ Do not regard your servant as a worthless woman, for all along I have been speaking out of my great anxiety and vexation." ¹⁷ Then Eli answered, "Go in peace, and the God of Israel grant your petition that you have made to him." ¹⁸ And she said, "Let your servant find favor in your eyes." Then the woman went her way and ate, and her face was no longer sad.
1 Samuel 1:12-18 ESV

In this passage where Eli the priest sees Hannah praying, she is mouthing words he can't hear, and Eli thinks that she must be drunk. In today's context, the scene would be as though Eli saw a small news clip from someone's speech and drew a conclusion out of the little bit that he was able to see. Have you ever observed someone pray, or maybe someone giving a speech and, like Eli, thought that the person might not entirely be in their best state of mind? Or have you ever fallen prey to some fancy video or audio editing tricks that highlight a brief clip of a bigger event, and from that small piece out of a bigger picture you cast judgement on a person or group of people, and maybe even threw in your own bit of opinion through social media? Perhaps later on, you learned more about the larger event from where the edited clip was taken and realized you allowed yourself to have your perception manipulated, and you cast your judgement too quickly.

Many of us have fallen victim to similar situations of knee-jerk judgements arising from lack of understanding of what we initially perceived. I especially appreciate God's reminder to us in the book of Proverbs on this subject saying, *"Don't*

jump to conclusions—there may be a perfectly
good explanation for what you just saw."[20]

As with most things, the best way to understand specific situations is by first knowing the context. In this passage, it's easy for us as readers to think of Eli as being too judgmental and unfair toward Hannah. He thought she was a drunk woman based merely on the fact that her manner of praying may have been "weird" to him. Nonetheless, the context of this passage shows us the state of the nation of Israel at the time, which informed Eli's thoughts upon seeing Hannah praying at the temple.

In those days, not everyone in Israel was living a godly life. In fact, many were living outright despicable lives. This was the time when Judges led the people of Israel. While there were great and memorable judges like Deborah, Gideon, and Samson, the nation was in a state of moral decline. *"In those days there was no king in Israel. Everyone did what was right in his own eyes."*[21] Eli was one of the last of Israel's judges, yet even his own sons were living evil, morally questionable, ungodly lives.

---

[20] Proverbs 25:8 *The Message*
[21] Judges 21:25

"*...the sons of Eli were worthless men. They did not know the Lord.*"[22] As Eli was sitting by the entrance, we see that part of his work was making sure order was kept in the temple, which explains why he was keeping a close eye on Hannah. Within this historical setting and Israel's moral condition, loitering drunkards and vagrants may not have been an uncommon sight at the temple. It would not have been illogical for Eli to assume that Hannah may be one of these people.

It may seem like the story is abbreviated a bit, but we see that Eli has the good and godly sense of a true judge of Israel to see and understand Hannah's situation soon after she explained herself to him. Thus, while I may have spent some time looking at Eli's character, the story still effectively communicates how God hears Hannah's prayer. In this instance, Eli was used by God to minister to Hannah and assure her that He has heard her prayer, even if Eli seems to not have immediately perceived it. God is seemingly saying to Hannah that neither her inaudible words nor how others perceive her prayer is relevant, because God heard her *speaking*

---

[22] 1 Samuel 2:12

in her heart,[23] and He will answer.

Like Eli, we may look in judgement at others around us based on what's currently going on around us. Indeed, *"what you see and what you hear depends a great deal on where you are standing. It also depends on what sort of person you are."*[24] It stands to reason then, that we should devote ourselves to becoming the sort of people who are godly, so that our perception remains not just clear but also loving, compassionate, and wise.

Sometimes praying in public, or in the presence of other people can make us feel uncomfortable but, like Hannah, our focus when we pray truly needs to be only on the One to whom our prayers are being sent. God hears our prayers in our hearts, in private, in public, in our times of joy, and in our times of desperation. People watching may not understand, but what matters is God listens and understands, and He answers.

---

[23] 1 Samuel 1:13
[24] C.S. Lewis, *The Magician's Nephew*

Think: Though our judgement of others may be flawed, like Eli's, God can use us to bring assurance and comfort that God hears and answers prayer.

Pray: Lord, please give me wisdom to have words to say to encourage others, just as you used Eli to encourage Hannah. And may I, like Hannah, always remember that you hear the prayers of our hearts.

----------- ooo -----------

Miracles in the mundane

> [19] *They rose early in the morning and worshiped before the Lord; then they went back to their house at Ramah. And Elkanah knew Hannah his wife, and the Lord remembered her.* [20] *And in due time Hannah conceived and bore a son, and she called his name Samuel, for she said, "I have asked for him from the Lord."*
> *1 Samuel 1:19-20 ESV*

I have learned from my experience as a mother of teens that waiting is not only hard for my children, but it is sometimes also hard for me. This year is my second time going through the period of waiting for results of college applications with my child. Admittedly, it has become a little bit more bearable this time with our daughter Hannah, than it was the first time with our eldest son, Jonah. I have found three things that are consistently helpful during the time of waiting: 1. Prayer, 2. trust in God, and 3. living life. While none of these are new or can be considered earth-shattering insight, it helps to remind myself that I need only to pray, trust in God, and keep going with everyday life, especially during those times when thinking about the future causes me to stay inside my own head.

As we move along the first chapter of 1 Samuel, we come to this part where, after Hannah has been praying and crying her heart out to the Lord, she rises early with her husband to worship before they travel back home. After all her crying, praying, and her encounter with Eli the priest assuring her that God heard her prayer, Hannah knows that it's time to go back home and return to everyday life. Still, the first thing she did before going back home was to, once again, worship God with her family.

How unlike Hannah's life is the pace in which our lives now go. Even as Christians, we often are just so eager to get to the next thing that needs to be done that we forget to pause to pray and worship. Little do we realize that our hurried life need not be so rushed, because it is exactly when we are most anxious about something that it is most important for us to worship. Only in worshipping God can we most effectively remind ourselves of Who is really in control of the things that happen in our lives and be able to rest in his love and trust in His might.

As Hannah rested in the assurance of God's love and power to answer her prayer, God enabled her to once again find joy in her day-to-day life. We can assume that having her anxiety lifted away allowed Hannah to relate more effectively and lovingly to the people around her, and especially with her husband. In going about the seemingly "normal" and mundane things in her life, God answered Hannah's prayer and she was able to conceive a child.

How important it must have been for Hannah to not be anxious in order for her to rekindle the romance with her husband despite any past hurts, for her to be in good health, and ultimately, in order for her to bear a son! Hannah's consistent worship, prayer, and trust in God relieved her of disabling anxiety. What a tremendous reminder this is for everyone who is anxious today, of how essential prayer and worship are to effectively be relating with those around us as we wait, and seeing miracles happen in our lives.

Often, God answers our prayers through the course of what we might consider to be just ordinary activities or events in our lives. Hannah and Elkanah may have just been going about what they would normally do, but God was answering Hannah's prayer and granting her the miracle she had asked for.

Surely, Hannah was eagerly awaiting God's answer to her prayer, but she could not allow herself to wallow in sadness or worry while she waited. Neither could she put her life on hold. She continued to worship God and nurture her relationships. Her relationships both with God and with her husband grew while she waited for God's answer to her prayer.

Think: In what ways might anxieties steal joy and health from you and the most important relationships in your life? Decide today to put God first. Worship Him and trust that He is working in your life to make everything work together for your good and for His glory.

Pray: Lord, thank you that you have heard my prayers. Please enable me to worship you while I wait and help me to see your miracles in my life and praise you every day.

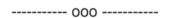

----------- ooo -----------

Purposeful preparation

*21 The man Elkanah and all his house went up to
offer to the Lord the yearly sacrifice and to pay
his vow. 22 But Hannah did not go up, for she
said to her husband, "As soon as the child is
weaned, I will bring him, so that he may appear
in the presence of the Lord and dwell there
forever." 23 Elkanah her husband said to her, "Do
what seems best to you; wait until you have
weaned him; only, may the Lord establish his
word."
1 Samuel 1:21-23   ESV*

Going to church and sitting through a worship service can sometimes be uncomfortable. Each attendee might identify their own *favorite-* as well as *least-favorite-part-of-the-program* based on the level of ease (or unease) that they feel at each portion of the service. When I was much younger, I often felt most uncomfortable during the offering. As the plate was passed down each row, I felt a knot in my stomach getting tighter as the plate got closer to where I was sitting. Thankfully, on some Sundays when I would be sitting next to my grandmother, she would pull out a bill or two from her purse and hand it to me so that I would have something to put in the offering plate. Praise the Lord for godly grandmothers! During those precious Sundays, not only did my dear grandmother ease my anxiety, more importantly, she helped me learn a valuable lesson about worshipping God through giving.

I learned that it makes a difference in my worship experience when I come to church prepared to give. As a little girl, it relieved my anxiety, knowing that I was able to participate in worship. As an adult, giving allowed me to experience the joy that comes from knowing that all I have comes from God, and when I give, I am able to thank Him for entrusting me with all that He has given. It glorifies God when I give my tithes and offerings because I acknowledge His lordship, care, and sustaining power over my life.

As we approach the end of the first chapter of 1 Samuel, we see that the Lord has given Hannah the child that she had so earnestly prayed and asked God for. God had graciously given her a baby boy, Samuel, and entrusted her with his care. Hannah promised God that she would offer her child back to God to serve Him in the temple, and in these final verses of Chapter 1 we see her preparing her offering. Hannah said to her husband, *"As soon as the child is weaned, I will bring him, so that he may appear in the presence of the Lord and dwell there forever."*

Hannah's commitment to the Lord is seen in how she followed through on her promise to God. In joyful obedience, not only did Hannah keep her promise, she also made sure that she had completely done her part to ensure that she did not merely make an offering. Hannah prepared her offering and made sure that God received her best. How glad it must have made God's heart to see such purposeful preparation of Hannah's offering!

When we go to worship in God's house, with God's family, the preparation that we take throughout the week to ensure that we offer our best to the Lord makes a difference in our worship experience. It also makes a difference in the worship experience of those around us. We bless the Lord's name and give Him glory when we acknowledge His work in our lives and thank Him for sustaining, providing, and enabling us to give.

Think: How can I best prepare my gifts in order to worshipfully give an offering that is pleasing to God?

Pray: Lord, thank you that you give me all I need in order that I may give back to you. Help me to not take anything for granted, but to always prepare purposefully in order to present an offering that pleases you. Amen.

----------- ooo -----------

Heard
Reflections on the story of Hannah

Promise-keeping

24 And when she had weaned him, she took him up with her, along with a three-year-old bull, an ephah of flour, and a skin of wine, and she brought him to the house of the Lord at Shiloh. And the child was young. 25 Then they slaughtered the bull, and they brought the child to Eli. 26 And she said, "Oh, my lord! As you live, my lord, I am the woman who was standing here in your presence, praying to the Lord. 27 For this child I prayed, and the Lord has granted me my petition that I made to him. 28 Therefore I have lent him to the Lord. As long as he lives, he is lent to the Lord."

And he worshiped the Lord there."

1 Samuel 1:24-28 ESV

If you have ever earnestly prayed and asked God for something, asked others to pray with you, and waited a long time for God's answer, then you'll be able to relate to Hannah. You will also be able to better understand and imagine how thankful she must have been when she finally received the long-awaited answer to her prayers. Hannah was abundantly thankful, and we can see just how thankful she was by how she took great care in preparing her offerings as she got ready to go and worship in the house of the Lord.

Hannah not only prepared her offerings physically, but she also prepared her heart. I can imagine a bit of emotional confusion in Hannah as she acknowledged God's power, faithfulness, and kindness to her in allowing her to bear a son, while also feeling a bit of unease in her heart as she anticipated their parting. She reveled in God's love and might, while wrestling with the natural desire a mother would have to keep her child close to her.

I suppose this is similar with the way I feel about my own children. While I marvel at the wonderful things that God has done and is preparing them to do, I also can't help but feel the tugging in my heart whenever it comes time to say goodbye. I want to keep them close, but I also know that I have dedicated them to God when they were young, and from that point forward, acknowledged that God can take them, mold them, and prepare them to serve Him in whatever way He sees best.

God, in His perfect wisdom, knew Hannah's heart. He heard the quiet sobs of this loving mother, even before she knew she was going to be able to conceive and bear a child! In His loving wisdom, God surrounded Hannah with just the right people to help her at every stage of her life as a mother. Two of these people were Elkanah, her husband and Eli, the priest.

Being Elkanah's wife, having to go with him to make the yearly pilgrimage to Shiloh enabled Hannah to grow in her worship and personal relationship with God. Then, meeting Eli the priest during one of these trips, God gave Hannah someone to whom she can be accountable. Having met Eli and telling him about what she had been praying to God for, Hannah was able to tell someone about her promise. In so doing, she opened the door for another person to see whether she would keep her promise. What encouragement Hannah must have felt as she said to Eli, "*Sir, do you remember me?... I am the very woman who stood here several years ago... I asked the Lord to give me this boy, and he has granted my request. Now I am giving him to the Lord, and he will belong to the Lord his whole life.*"[25]

God in His wisdom surrounded Hannah with the right people at the right time to strengthen her. Promise-keeping can be a challenge when it comes time to deliver on our word, but if our promise is made with joy and humility, God empowers us to do as we say. As God's children, we know this to be true not only when we make a promise to God, but also when we give our word to others. As He is our God who keeps His word, He is also the God who we can trust to enable us to maintain our own integrity. As He did with Hannah, we can trust that God has been molding us, and giving us everything we need to become the people He needs us to be. He surrounds us, His children, with people who will help us grow and to whom we can be accountable.

---

[25] 1 Samuel 1:26-28a *New Living Translation*

Think: Does my promise-keeping reflect my trust in the faithfulness and integrity of my God?

Pray: Lord, you know how keeping my word to you and to others can sometimes become difficult. I thank you that you give me all that I need to overcome any and all challenges to my integrity, and I know that I can trust you to enable me to always keep my word. Amen.

----------- ooo -----------

Heard
Reflections on the story of Hannah

Heart, horn, mouth

¹ And Hannah prayed and said,
"My heart exults in the Lord;
my horn is exalted in the Lord.
My mouth derides my enemies,
because I rejoice in your salvation."
And he worshiped the Lord there."
1 Samuel 2:1   ESV

Hannah prayed a long time for a child. Her prayers had been filled with tears. She pleaded with God year after year. She waited a long time for God's answer. When God came through with His miraculous response to Hannah's long-desired request, we can only imagine what overwhelming joy and thankfulness may have overcome her. Perhaps the joy she felt can be compared to seeing a loved one come home after a long absence – like the heart that leaps inside the child whose father had been deployed to war and is now finally arriving at the airport. The joy takes the form of tears, and the energy inside explodes into a sprint and a jump into the arms of her long-awaited hero.

There are three aspects of joy that this first verse of Hannah's prayer captures. The first has to do with *internal exultation*. Hannah's joy begins in her heart, with a recognition that it is God who put it there. She says, "**my heart** exults in the Lord." Hannah acknowledges the power of God in hearing her prayers and realizes that it is only in God that such unspeakable joy is possible. While this type of joy is one that others may not be able to fully comprehend and share with Hannah, it is nonetheless tremendous, and she treasures it in her heart, and personally worships the Lord.

The second aspect of Hannah's joy is *public recognition*. As Hannah struggled inwardly during the years that she prayed and waited for God's answer, she also dealt with the public ridicule of those around her. She was bullied and hurt, even by those who were close to her. Now that the Lord has answered her prayer, not only does she feel joy in her heart, but she is also publicly vindicated. Hannah rejoices in the honor that could only come from God's mighty work in her life. Hannah says, "**my horn** is exalted in the Lord." As in Psalm 18:2, horn symbolizes God's strength and dignity.[26] Like Hannah, we can be sure that God, our loving Father and sovereign judge, will fairly bring justice to all. Justice comes by God's hand and will when we fully trust in Him. What joy and reassurance it brings to us, His children, when we are vindicated in God's perfect time. In our hearts we experience the joy of God's answer, and in our lives others see God's wondrous work.

---

[26] Moody Bible Commentary, p. 405

Finally, the profound working of God that Hannah felt inwardly, and seen by others outwardly, has found its way to being announced publicly. Hannah found joy not just in private exultation, or in the personal vindication, but also in publicly proclaiming God's awesome goodness. "**My mouth** derides my enemies, because I rejoice in your salvation," says Hannah. Nothing can cause greater derision to those who oppose God than when His children speak of His goodness and salvation. In rejoicing publicly, Hannah not only expressed her joy, but also proclaimed and exalted God.

In all this rejoicing, it is important to note that Hannah acknowledged that the source of her overwhelming joy was God, not Samuel who was given in answer to her prayer. In realizing this, Hannah's joy remained and was not diminished even a little, even when it was time to let Samuel go. Hannah's joy was anchored on God.

In our own lives, there may be times that we experience long periods of waiting for God to act upon our prayers. Yet, sometimes, when we finally receive God's answer, we fail to acknowledge the true source of the joy that we are finally able to experience. The joy of receiving something from the hand of God can only be fully felt when we allow the joy in our hearts to bubble over to a public recognition of our almighty, loving heavenly Father, from whom all blessings flow.

Think: Do your heart, your horn, and your mouth all agree in exalting and proclaiming the true source of your joy?

Pray: Teach me Lord to rejoice always in You -- the only true source of lasting joy, justice, and salvation. Amen.

----------- ooo -----------

Perfect

² *There is none holy like the Lord:*
  for there is none besides you;
  there is no rock like our God.
³ *Talk no more so very proudly,*
  let not arrogance come from your mouth;
for the Lord is a God of knowledge,
  and by him actions are weighed.
⁴ *The bows of the mighty are broken,*
  but the feeble bind on strength.
⁵ *Those who were full have hired themselves out*
for bread,
  but those who were hungry have ceased to
hunger.
The barren has borne seven,
  but she who has many children is forlorn."
1 Samuel 2:2-5   ESV

When I was in college in the Philippines, I had the rare privilege of being classmates with a beauty queen. It was the '80s, and she literally won a national beauty contest that was broadcast on television and printed in the frontpage of every major daily in the country, with a picture of her wearing her crown and holding a scepter. This young woman not only had a pretty face. Her complexion was clear. Her figure looked perfectly proportioned. She was tall and slim yet still shapely. She had perfect teeth, and a smile that could light up a room. As if that wasn't enough to cause feelings of insecurity in all the other young women in school, this model of rare beauty was also quite personable. She was friendly to everyone even though she came from a wealthy family. To top it all off, she was also very witty and smart – making it into the university's dean's list every single semester. In my young mind, she was the closest thing to "perfection" that I had seen and met.

This memory of my beauty-queen classmate comes to mind as I ponder this passage in Samuel where Hannah speaks about God and how there is none like Him. "There is none **holy** like the Lord," declared Hannah. This means God is *exalted or* *worthy of complete devotion as one perfect in goodness and righteousness.*[27] God is perfect. In every way that I can see or imagine, and even in ways that I cannot fully comprehend, God is perfect. Hannah's song in 1 Samuel puts emphasis on God's holiness and perfection as it repeats this point three times in the same verse. Why this emphasis on God's perfection?

Seeing the holiness and perfection of God gives all of us a proper perspective of our imperfection. God's holiness is the cure for the greatest ailments of man's heart. Understanding God's perfection rids us of pride, assures us of justice, and fills us with hope. There is nothing as humbling as coming face-to-face with one who is perfect in every way—the One who is strongest, wisest, most beautiful – that is God. He is all-knowing, all-seeing, all-hearing, all-loving. He will judge all according to His perfect justice – that is God. We can always depend on Him because He always keeps His Word. We can have hope that is secure because of who God is. This is God.

---

[27] "holy," Merriam-Webster.com Dictionary, https://www.merriam-webster.com/dictionary/holy. Accessed 2/19/2020.

So, while we can meet people who may seem to come close to perfection in some way, we know that they will never be perfect in every way. None of us will ever even come close to God's perfection. Because God alone is perfectly wise, Hannah's song implores us to speak humbly—to *"talk no more so very proudly, let not arrogance come from your mouth."*

Because God is perfectly just, He alone can make reversals of circumstances and situations happen -- in society and in our own lives. God alone has the moral authority to justify reversals of fortune in this life, and so we need to trust His judgment. He breaks the weapons of those who think themselves powerful while He gives strength to the weak. He can give wealth to the hardworking person and take away riches from those who think they have an endless supply.[28]

Hannah celebrates God's holiness and His mighty power by reminding us of her own life's complete reversal. Her life was once seemingly tragic, but it changed when God intervened. She was barren but became blessed with a household of children.

---

[28] 1 Samuel 2:3-5

While Peninah, the woman who bullied and oppressed her, became sad and forgotten.

Meeting people whom we may think of as being so close to perfection should make us thankful to God. Seen through the lens of God's holiness and His Word, God allows us a glimpse of how great He alone can be, and the great work that He can do in the lives of those who find their trust, hope, and salvation in Him. Indeed, Hannah's song always rings true -- "*There is none holy like the Lord: for there is none besides you; there is no rock like our God.*"

Think: God's holiness is our
assurance that we can depend on
Him for with our lives. He is our hope,
our strength, and our salvation.

Pray: You are awesome, Lord! There
is none like you. Thank you for
allowing me to see my life and my
world in the light of your holiness and
find hope and salvation in you.

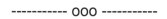

----------- ooo -----------

Sovereign

⁶ *The Lord kills and brings to life;*
   he brings down to Sheol and raises up.
⁷ *The Lord makes poor and makes rich;*
   he brings low and he exalts.
⁸ *He raises up the poor from the dust;*
   he lifts the needy from the ash heap
to make them sit with princes
   and inherit a seat of honor.
For the pillars of the earth are the Lord's,
   and on them he has set the world."
1 Samuel 2:6-8   ESV

It is tempting to jump right into this portion of Hannah's prayer in the light of issues and problems we may see around us today. Even as I write this section, much talk about the presidential elections fill the headlines of mainstream and social media. There are injustices that need fixing and community concerns that need addressing. If we take what we see in the news as we read these verses, we might say it is a commentary on our present society.

Indeed, only the Lord can bring justice to the oppressed, restore those who have been wronged, and raise up leaders as He pleases. While these points are true, these verses must also be read within the context of the entire prayer of Hannah and what we have learned about her life so far. In taking time to step back to shine a light on the context we will gain further insight on how it applies to our lives and our world.

Hannah's exultation comes from a very personal experience. She may have once viewed herself as lowly, needy, and dead in a way that she was unable to bring forth life (vv. 6-8), as low as the garbage that sits in the ash heap; but now she exalts in God's power which raised her up from the

lowliest places in her heart that only God could see.
Yet even as she revisits the lows and highs of her
life, she recognizes that nothing happens without
God's say-so. This is God's sovereignty. *"The Lord
makes poor and makes rich; he brings low and he
exalts."* (v.7) No matter what station she found
herself in life, God remains God.

After seeing what these verses may have meant to
Hannah who prayed this prayer, we can better
appreciate how they apply to our own lives. As we
journeyed with Hannah in her lowest valleys and
related to her as we recalled low points in our own
lives, we gained an understanding of how God is
there even through life's uncertainties. We
understood what it means to rejoice even in
darkness.

When we can't see what's ahead, we are unable to
prepare ourselves for what's to come. This lack of
control over things in our lives can cause us to feel
frightened and insecure. It is in these times that
knowing God as sovereign, as almighty and as all-
knowing gives us the most comfort. Thank God for
the moments of darkness that He allows in our lives
as it is sometimes the only way we can truly
appreciate His watchful care and power in lives.

Without acknowledging God's sovereignty in our own lives, it would be impossible to truly understand God's sovereignty over our world. The power that God allows us to see working in our lives is the same power that God has over all the earth. Over every nation, over every government, over everything, God is sovereign.

I recall a conversation I had with my sister one day. We were talking about our health concerns and she said something in that conversation which I think lines up perfectly with Hannah's prayer here. She said, "we might think that we own our bodies, but really, all of it belongs to God. He is in control." And as it is true with us, it is true in the world, just like Hannah says in her prayer. The "pillars of the earth" or the leaders of the world[29] are the Lord's whether they recognize His lordship or not. He sets them in their place to bring stability to the nations (just as pillars make structures stable[30]) according to His wisdom and for His pleasure.

God is sovereign over the whole world, and over our own lives. His Lordship remains true whether

---

[29] Charles Ryrie commentary on 1 Samuel 2:8, © 1978
[30] Moody commentary, p. 407, © 2014

people call Him Lord or choose to deny He even exists. God is God no matter what happens or who chooses to believe; and what joy there is for us when we acknowledge Him as our Lord. When we see who truly is in control of the world, we find joy and comfort in knowing that we can rest in the hands of the all-knowing, all-powerful God.

Think: God takes down and lifts up whomever He so chooses, and His choices are always best.

Pray: Lord, grant me the faith and peace to trust and rest, knowing that you are in control. You are God, no matter the circumstances, and I will find joy in praising you.

----------- OOO -----------

Sarah and Hannah

⁹ He will guard the feet of his faithful ones,
but the wicked shall be cut off in darkness,
for not by might shall a man prevail.
¹⁰ The adversaries of the Lord shall be broken to pieces;
against them he will thunder in heaven.
The Lord will judge the ends of the earth;
he will give strength to his king
and exalt the horn of his anointed."
1 Samuel 2:9-10   ESV

Throughout all of scripture, from Genesis to Revelation, the entire Bible is undoubtedly a unified book about Jesus. From the story of creation in Genesis, to the prophecies revealed to the Apostle John in the book of Revelation, God's plan of restoring man to Himself through Jesus' sacrifice is communicated. It has been said that there is a *scarlet thread* that runs throughout scripture.[31] Passages can be found throughout the Old Testament which were messianic in nature, because they spoke of Jesus and the blood He would shed, his triumph over evil, and the salvation of His people, hundreds of years before he came in human form as a child born in Bethlehem.

This part of Hannah's song is an example of an Old Testament passage that expressly refers to Jesus even before his incarnation. Curiously, if not magnificently, Hannah speaks here of God giving *strength to his king*, even though it was years before Israel's first king is even chosen or named. Also, she sings of a King who will ultimately defeat the adversaries of the Lord. Hannah seems to be

---

[31] *The Scarlet Thread Through the Bible*, W.A. Criswell

given a special prophetic message which she shares in her rejoicing, and which she proclaims unashamedly even before anything around her gave any indication of such things coming to pass. Hannah's experience of having to trust completely by faith that God will do as he says, even though there is nothing she can immediately see to confirm it, is very similar to the story of Sarah, the wife of Abraham.

As with Sarah, God chose to reveal holy truth and divine promises to Hannah who was at first scorned but was later vindicated by His power. Like Sarah, Hannah was barren. Yet out of each of their barren wombs God caused sons to be born who would later prove to be instrumental in establishing the kingly line from which our Messiah and victorious king of Kings would be born.

Many years before Hannah, God heard the prayer of Sarah, who thought she was too old to bear children. God had promised Abraham that through him and Sarah would come a great nation. Even when Sarah at times was not sure how this could possibly happen so late in their as-yet-childless marriage, God reached out to Sarah and showed

Himself to be the unchanging, faithful, and almighty God that He has always been and forever will be. The birth of Abraham and Sarah's child, and the great nation that would later form through him, could only happen by the power of God. For indeed, as Hannah later sang in her song, "*not by might shall a man prevail.*"

In Genesis 18, an encounter between the Lord, Abraham, and Sarah, was not exactly Sarah's shining moment. Sarah laughed at the thought of bearing a child in her old age.[32] Nonetheless, even her momentary questioning unmistakably shows us the truth about God that we have seen all along in this book. God hears our hearts. Just as God heard Sarah's heart yearning for a child, He also heard it when, for a moment, she could not fathom how from her old and worn out body a great nation can still come. God hears all that our heart says, whether it's joy or sorrow, belief or doubt. He hears and responds to us even when we don't fully understand. He asks, "*Is there anything too hard for the Lord?*"[33] The question may appear rhetorical,

---

[32] Genesis 18:10
[33] Genesis 18:14a

and yet, it often needs to be asked and answered for the sake of our own hearts.

At the end of the stories that were recorded in the Bible for both Sarah and Hannah, both were blessed to have seen the wonderful way that God hears and answers prayer. Each of them asked for a child, and each rejoiced in seeing the answer to that prayer. But more than that, God revealed to both women things that were yet to come. Neither Sarah nor Hannah saw within their lifetimes the fulfillment of everything that the Lord allowed them to know that would happen in the future. Yet both of these women found the true source of their fulfillment and joy in the Lord, and both left a legacy of faith to those who would follow after them.

Sarah's legacy of faith is mentioned in the New Testament in the book of Hebrews along with others who "died in faith, not having received the things promised, but having seen them and greeted them from afar."[34] *"By faith Sarah herself received power to conceive, even when she was past the age, since she considered him faithful who had*

---

[34] Hebrews 11:13

promised. Therefore from one man, and him as good as dead, were born descendants as many as the stars of heaven and as many as the innumerable grains of sand by the seashore."[35]

Truly, in the end, it was not the state of their country, their families, or even the state of their own physical bodies that mattered. Neither did it matter whether they were able to immediately see the fulfillment of all that God promised. The stories of Hannah and Sarah show us that God hears us, He answers us, and He always keeps His word.

---

[35] Hebrews 11:11-12

Think: "*… without faith it is impossible to please him, for whoever would draw near to God must believe that he exists and that he rewards those who seek him.*" Hebrews 11:6

Pray: Lord, please grow in me the kind of faith that is like Sarah's and Hannah's. Thank you for all the answers to prayer that I have experienced, and for the fulfillment of all your promises that are yet to come.

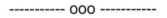

----------- ooo -----------

Heard
Reflections on the story of Hannah

God heard

> *11 Then Elkanah went home to Ramah. And the boy was ministering to the Lord in the presence of Eli the priest."*
> *1 Samuel 2:11   ESV*

It had been a seemingly long and arduous road for Hannah. The years of praying for a son, enduring the sneers and bullying of people around her, seeing another woman bear children for her husband… the days may have seemed endless, but her heart did not tire of praying and trusting in the Lord's grace and mighty power. She had heard the stories of barren women in Israel's history and she believed in the same God who promised to give them children and delivered on that promise. Hannah knew this God of Israel and she trusted Him, until she saw her prayers answered and discovered that her true joy was not actually in becoming a mother, but it was in experiencing first-hand the power and love of her Mighty God.

What a great testimony of faith this unfolding story of Hannah must have been for Elkanah to witness. As Hannah's husband, he is a silent character for most of the passages that we have read and studied. Nonetheless, the Lord saw it fit to mention his name once again as we come to the end of Hannah's story, and the focus goes back to the larger story of the nation of Israel. Elkanah was with Hannah as she first began praying for a child, and he is here once again as they offer back to God the child that He blessed them with.

From where we now stand we see Hannah and Elkanah, by virtue of Elkanah's family line, both played a major role in the history of Israel. Their son Samuel would be the last judge and will be used by God to choose Israel's first king. Did Elkanah know, as Hannah did, that Israel's kings, and later, the savior Jesus Christ, would come from the line to be established by God through His work with Samuel? Perhaps. But no matter how clearly or vaguely Elkanah's awareness was of things to come may have been, it is most important to note that he trusted God along with his wife. He was committed to his role as leader of his family. He encouraged in them the practice of prayer and worship, and he was there with Hannah to keep their promise to the Lord as they entrusted Samuel to him.

There is no detailed account of how the goodbyes may have gone between Samuel and his parents, but I imagine it to be joyous and not heart-wrenching. There may have been tears, but not of sadness. I think tears of joy, excitement, and great thankfulness to the Almighty God would have flowed freely as they said their goodbyes, and as they trusted that He who had allowed the birth of Samuel had great plans for their lives and for their nation.

Through the process of waiting, birthing, weaning, and then finally parting as they delivered their son as offering to God, Elkanah and Hannah may have also found great assurance even in the thought of the meaning of their names. Elkanah's name in Hebrew means '*God has made.*' Hannah's name translates from Hebrew to '*favor*' and '*grace*' in English. Their very names were constant reminders of the God who continues to care for them, who showers them with favor through his grace, and makes miracles happen by His great power. And as they named the son whom God had made, Samuel's name also serves as a reminder of the real relationship that God has with his children. Samuel means '*God heard.*'

In our own lives, God allows things to occur that reminds us not only of where we stand in Him, but also of who He is. Let's think about these events in our lives and consider what we could learn and remember about God through them. As this story and the names of Hannah, Elkanah, and Samuel remind us of our gracious creator who hears and answers our prayer, let's make it one of our life's goals to enable others to know and trust God through the story that we live out from one day to the next.

Think: You may not be named Elkanah (*God has made*), but you are surely made by God. Your name may not be Hannah (*favor, grace*) but God's generous love and grace reaches you, too. You may not have been named Samuel (*God heard*), but you can trust that God hears you.

Pray: I praise and thank you, God, for creating me, loving me, and hearing me. Thank you that nothing changes who you are no matter what circumstance or season of life I find myself in. Amen.

----------- ooo -----------

Made in the USA
Middletown, DE
03 July 2023

34528328R00064